UNDER the SEA

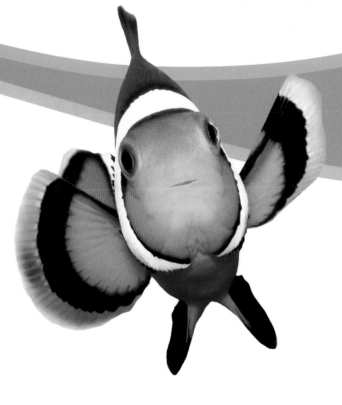

Sandy Creek
NEW YORK

An Imprint of Sterling Publishing
1166 Avenue of The Americas
New York, NY, 10036

Text © 2014 by QEB Publishing, Inc.
Illustrations © 2014 by QEB Publishing, Inc.

This 2014 edition published by Sandy Creek.

ISBN 978-1-4351-5536-7

Manufactured in Guangdong, China
Lot #:
4 6 8 10 9 7 5
05/16

Editors Sarah Eason and Victoria Garrard
Designed by Calcium and Austin Taylor
Art Director Laura Roberts-Jensen
Cover designer Rosie Levine

Words in **bold** can be found in the glossary on page 114.

UNDER the SEA

Sally Morgan and
Camilla de la Bédoyère

Sandy Creek
NEW YORK

Contents

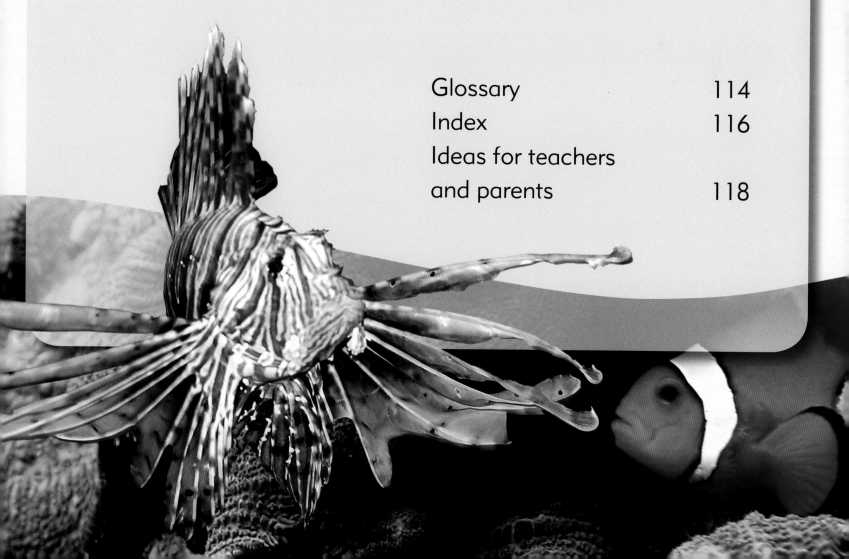

INTRODUCTION

The oceans and seas are huge areas of salty water.

Billions of animals live under the sea, from tiny shrimp to enormous blue whales.

Some ocean animals swim, while others float or crawl along the seabed.

Some ocean animals spend all their lives in the sea. Others spend time on land, too.

They look for food and mates, but they also look out for other animals that want to eat them!

There are five oceans. Together they make one world ocean.

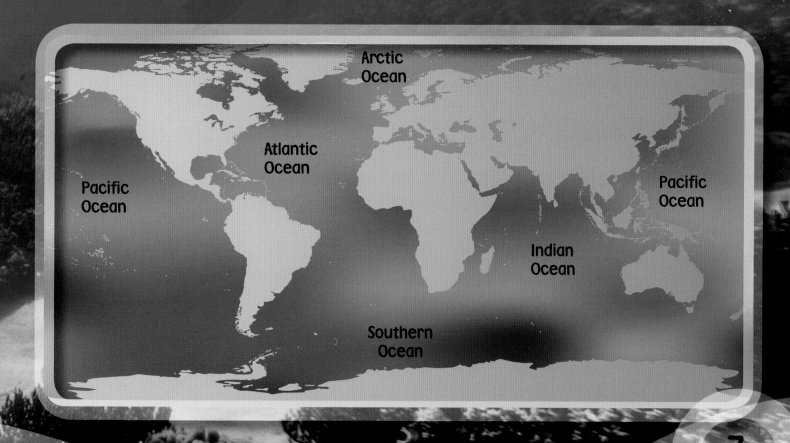

Arctic Ocean

Atlantic Ocean

Pacific Ocean

Pacific Ocean

Indian Ocean

Southern Ocean

Under the sea

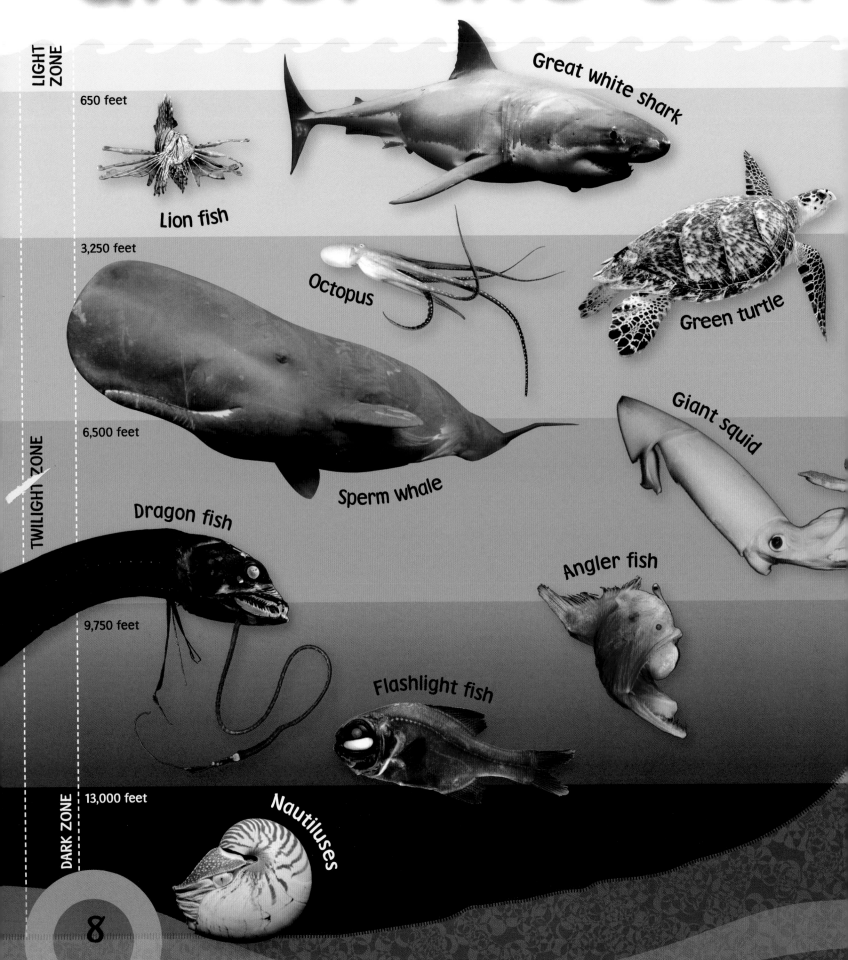

LIGHT ZONE

TWILIGHT ZONE

DARK ZONE

650 feet

3,250 feet

6,500 feet

9,750 feet

13,000 feet

Great white shark

Lion fish

Octopus

Green turtle

Giant squid

Sperm whale

Dragon fish

Angler fish

Flashlight fish

Nautiluses

8

Sunlight passes through seawater near the surface. Further down, the sunlight cannot get through, and the ocean becomes a deep, dark place—the **dark zone**.

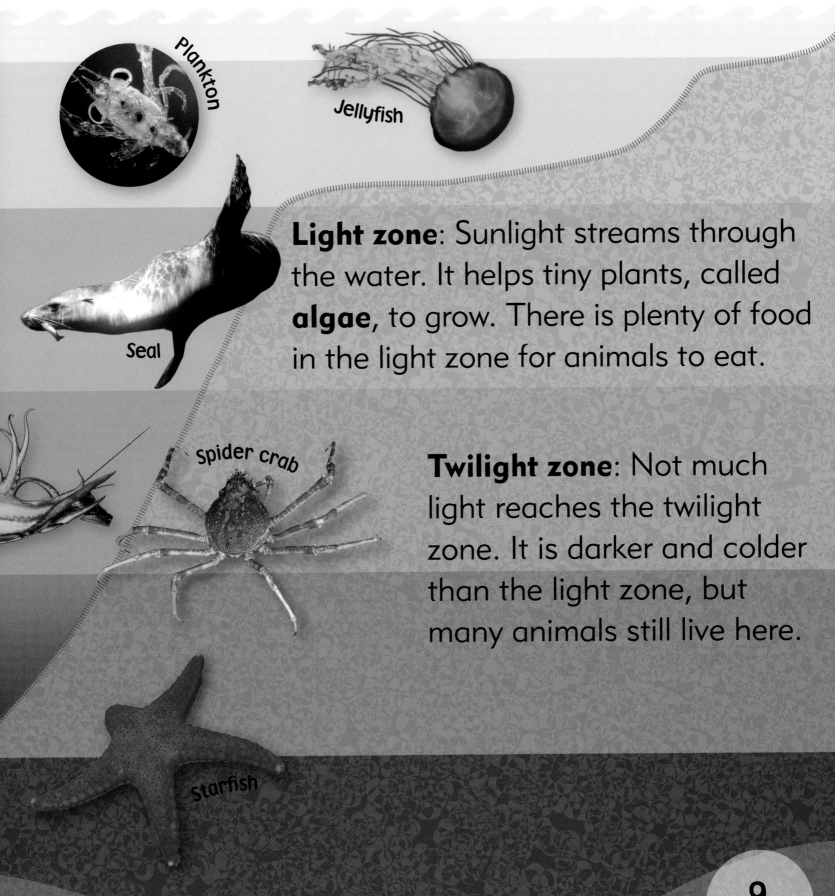

Plankton

Jellyfish

Seal

Light zone: Sunlight streams through the water. It helps tiny plants, called **algae**, to grow. There is plenty of food in the light zone for animals to eat.

spider crab

Twilight zone: Not much light reaches the twilight zone. It is darker and colder than the light zone, but many animals still live here.

Starfish

CORAL REEFS

A coral polyp can live for a hundred years.

There is a beautiful reef fish that snorts like a pig! It also has an incredible name—it's called the humuhumunukunukuāpua'a and it lives in the ocean around Hawaii.

Coral reefs have been on our planet for at least 230 million years, which means they shared the Earth with dinosaurs.

Box jellyfish are the world's deadliest jellyfish. They live around coral reefs in Southeast Asia.

The Great Barrier Reef is so big it can be seen from space!

Coral only grows where the water is clean. Dirty water kills coral polyps.

Some clownfish begin their lives as males, and then change into females!

Wrasses are coral fish that nibble at the skin and teeth of other fish to clean them.

Little blue-ringed octopuses change color, and their rings turn a deeper blue when they are angry. They also have a deadly bite.

Many sharks swim to coral reefs when it is time for them to give birth to their young. There are lots of places in a reef for the newborn pups to hide.

Coral reefs

Coral reefs look like beautiful underwater gardens. They are the home of many colorful animals, including fish, anemones, starfish, and even sea snakes.

More than one million different types of animal live on coral reefs.

The Great Barrier Reef is made up of more than 900 islands.

Coral reefs are found in warm water. Some reefs grow in shallow water near land. Others are separated from the land by a stretch of water. The Great Barrier Reef in Australia is the world's largest reef. It is more than 1,200 miles long.

Fish find plenty of food to eat on coral reefs.

Corals

Coral reefs are built by groups of tiny animals called hard **corals**. The corals have stony **skeletons**. When a hard coral dies, another coral grows on top of its skeleton. Over hundreds of years, the bony skeletons knit together to form the reef.

When a coral reef forms a circle, it is called an atoll.

14

Corals come in many shapes and colors. Hard corals can look like bubbles or trumpets. Some soft corals look like fans and gently sway in the warm waters.

Hard coral can look a little like a brain!

Small creatures can easily hide in colorful fan coral.

Clown fish

Sea anemones live on the reef. They have stinging **tentacles** that protect them from **predators**.

Most fish stay well away from sea anemones, but not the clown fish. The anemone's sting does not harm this brightly colored fish, so it makes its home between the anemone's tentacles.

Clown fish are covered in a layer of slime to protect them from the anemone's sting.

Whole families of clown fish can live in one anemone.

The clown fish also gets its food from the anemone. It eats the anemone's leftovers, such as shrimp. In return, the clown fish cleans the anemone's tentacles and scares away other fish.

Lionfish

Darting around the reef is the lionfish. It has a striking, stripy body. This fish may look beautiful, but the spines on its **fins** give a painful sting.

Lionfish sometimes hunt together in groups to catch their prey.

The lionfish's stripes warn predators to stay away.

Lionfish only use their stingers for defense. If another animal threatens it, the lionfish does not need to swim away. It can simply point its deadly spines toward the enemy.

Lionfish spread out their fins to catch prey.

Lionfish are hunters. They corner prey with their large fins before swallowing them in one gulp.

19

Reef sharks

With its wide jaws and jagged teeth, the reef shark is a fierce hunter. Most sharks have a slim body and a powerful tail fin, perfect for gliding through water.

Reef sharks have rows of deadly, jagged teeth.

Large flaps of skin make it difficult to spot the wobbegong shark on the seabed.

Sharks, such as the large black-tip reef shark and the small wobbegong shark, swim up and down the reef, on the lookout for fish and squid. They often hide in caves during the day and come out at night to hunt.

Sea slugs

Most sea slugs are the same size as garden slugs, but others are longer than a person's arm! Their bright colors warn other animals that they taste terrible.

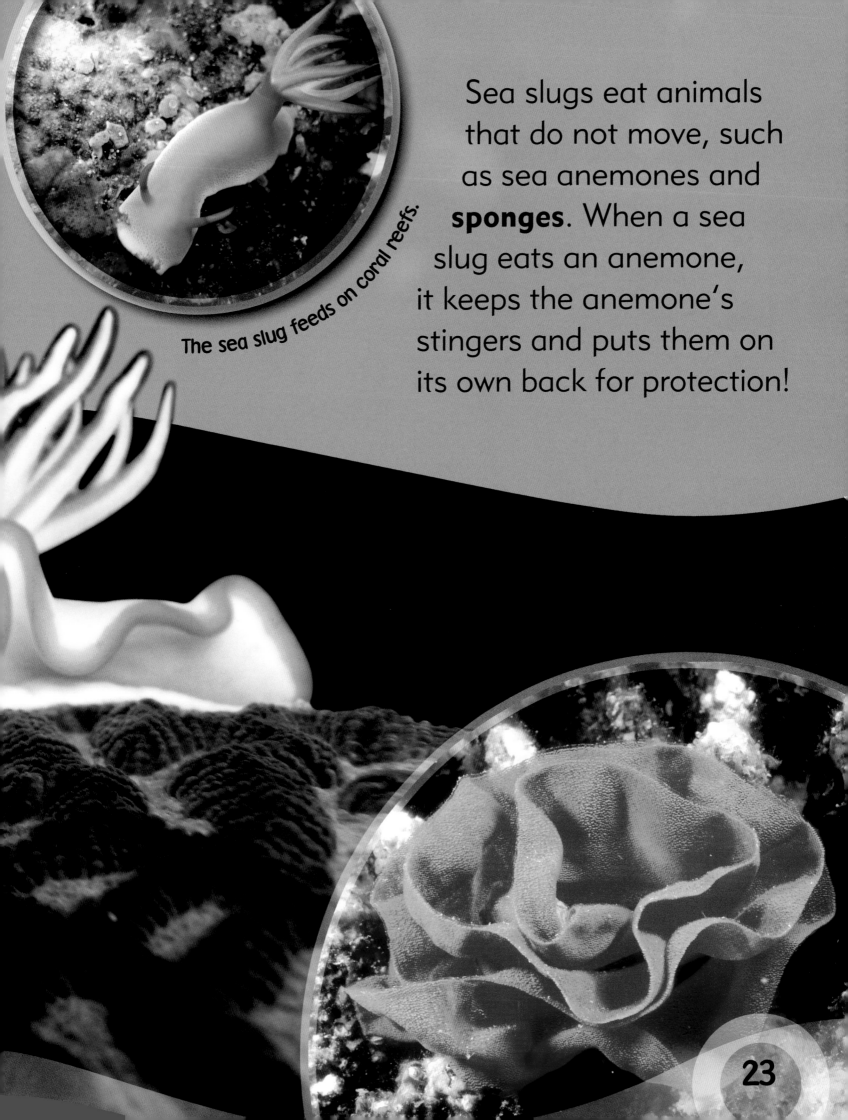

The sea slug feeds on coral reefs.

Sea slugs eat animals that do not move, such as sea anemones and **sponges**. When a sea slug eats an anemone, it keeps the anemone's stingers and puts them on its own back for protection!

Giant clams

Two huge shells protect
the giant clam's soft body.
It cannot move, so stays in
the same spot on the reef.

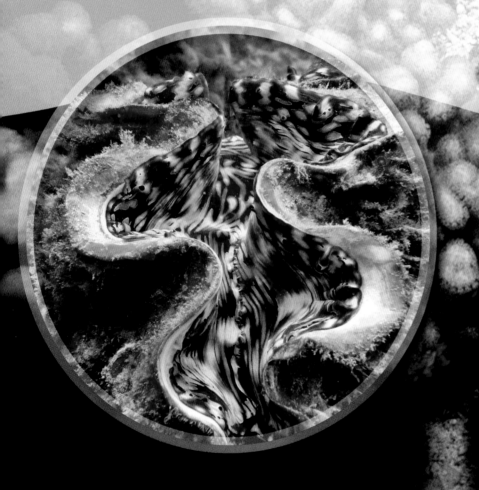

*If a clam senses danger,
it quickly closes its shells.*

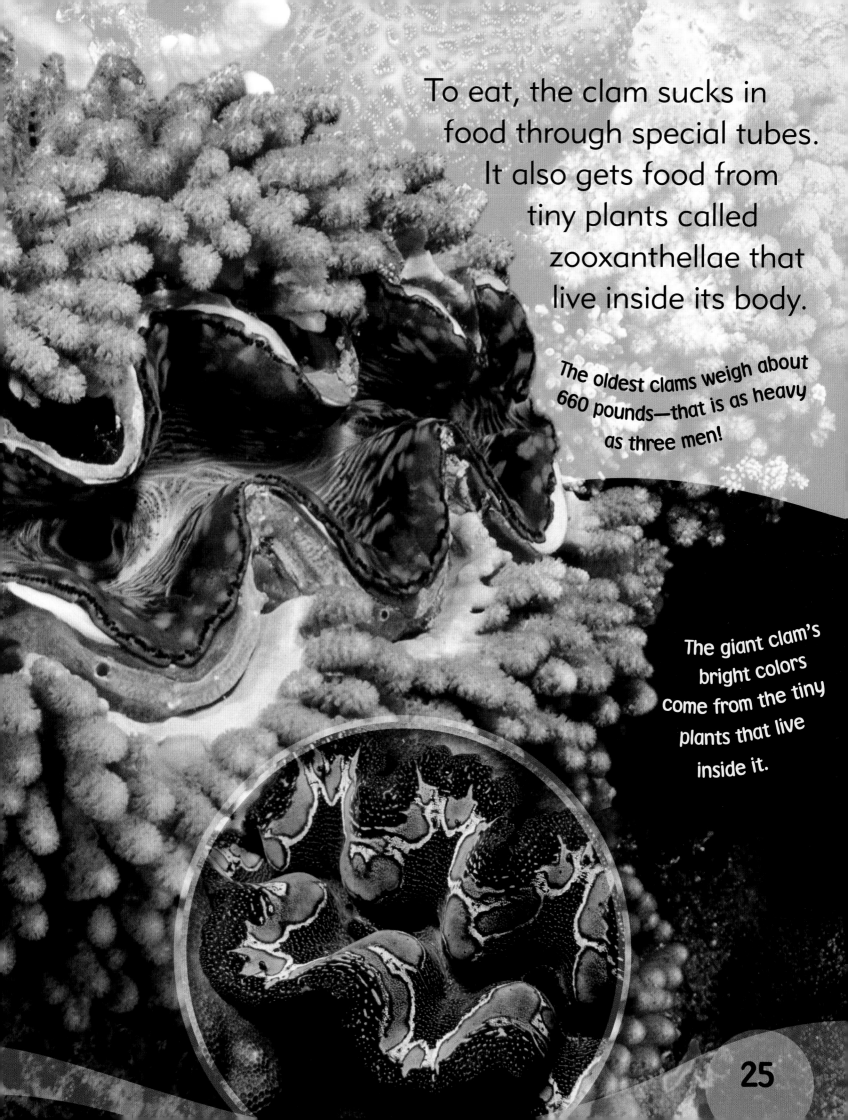

To eat, the clam sucks in food through special tubes. It also gets food from tiny plants called zooxanthellae that live inside its body.

The oldest clams weigh about 660 pounds—that is as heavy as three men!

The giant clam's bright colors come from the tiny plants that live inside it.

25

Cleaner shrimp

Little cleaner shrimp are busy coral animals. They like to pick off the tiny pests that live on fish, and eat them.

Cleaner shrimp have long skinny legs, and feelers that grow on their heads.

Up to 25 cleaner shrimp gather in one place where they wait for fish to come and see them. Sometimes they do a little "dance" to tell the fish they are ready to do their cleaning!

The place where cleaner shrimp gather is called a cleaning station.

Shrimp belong to the same family as crabs and lobsters.

Fan worms

Fan worms are worms that live on coral reefs. They have an amazing crown of sticky, colorful tentacles. They eat any animals that get trapped on them.

If a fan worm senses movement, it slides back into its tube.

Fan worms are also called feather duster worms.

A fan worm attaches itself to a rock and builds a hard tube around its body for protection. The tube is made from tiny grains of sand that are stuck together with sticky **mucus**.

The Christmas tree worm has bright tentacles that look like a Christmas tree.

Porcelain crabs

Porcelain crabs live inside a sea anemone's stinging tentacles. They don't get stung by the anemones.

Porcelain crabs are small and spotted.

The crab's front claws have feathery parts for trapping plankton in the water.

The crabs feed on tiny bits of food and plankton that float past them.

Their bodies are flat, so they can squeeze in between the tentacles. It's a good place to hide from other animals.

31

Green turtles

The sea turtle is an odd-looking **reptile**. It has scaly skin and most of its body is covered by a tough shell. It has a large, beaklike mouth that it uses to graze on sea plants.

The female green turtle digs a hole in the sand and lays her eggs in it.

Green turtles are often seen swimming in shallow water near the coast.

The newly hatched sea turtle makes its way to the sea.

Each year, female sea turtles return to the **beach** where they were born to lay their own eggs. About two months later, the eggs hatch. The tiny turtles dig their way out of the sand and dash to the water.

Tiger cowrie

This tiger cowrie is a large sea snail. It is egg-shaped and has a colorful shell that protects a soft body inside.

Cowries have one fleshy foot that they use to move around as they graze on tiny plants. Their shells are patterned and covered with a thin skin called a mantle.

At night, cowries crawl along the seabed of a coral reef.

Tiny "fingers" grow from the cowrie's mantle. They may help it breathe underwater.

When the animal dies, its shell may be washed up on the seashore.

Parrotfish

Pretty parrotfish are always changing the way they look. They can change both their colors and their patterns. Males can even change into females!

Much of the sand around a reef has come out of a parrotfish's body!

These fish nibble at coral, grinding its rocky parts into fine golden sand. They munch the coral to get to the soft polyps and little plants that live inside, and eat them.

There are about 80 types of parrotfish.

When a parrotfish goes to sleep it wraps itself up in slime, like a blanket.

Zebra moray

This snakelike animal slithers around a reef like a scaly reptile. In fact, it is a type of long-bodied fish called an eel.

Eels do not have any fins. Their bodies are covered with poisonous slime.

Zebra morays have black and white stripes, like a zebra. They attack other animals, and crush them with their powerful jaws and teeth.

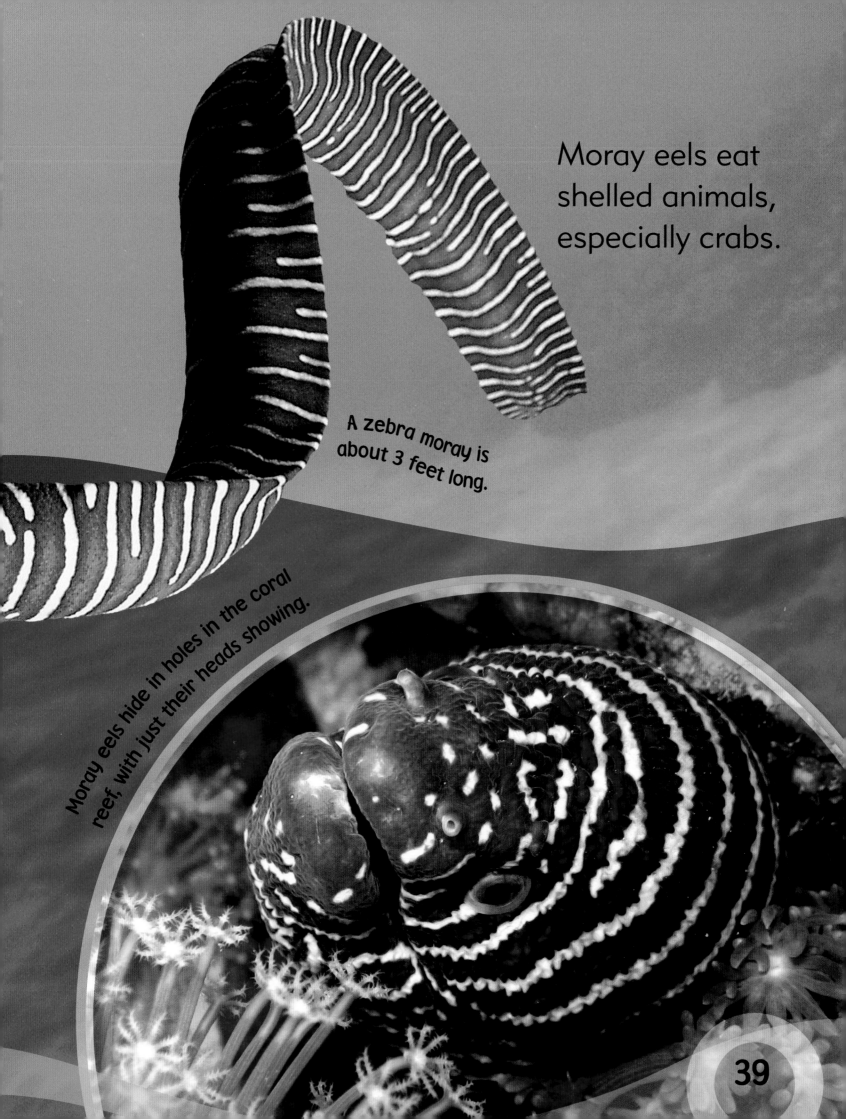

Moray eels eat shelled animals, especially crabs.

A zebra moray is about 3 feet long.

Moray eels hide in holes in the coral reef, with just their heads showing.

SHALLOW-WATER LIFE

Sunlight is made of many colors, but red light disappears in seawater. That's why everything looks blue or gray in shallow water.

Giant kelp can grow to 100 feet long, at a rate of 20 inches a day.

The largest starfish is called a brisingid. It can measure more than 4 feet across.

Crabs can run fast because they run sideways. They have ten legs, but usually use only four or six legs to run.

A sea urchin's mouth is on its bottom!

Horseshoe crabs have nine eyes and blue blood.

Furry little sea otters often cuddle or hold hands when they float in the ocean.

During a high tide, water gets deeper at the seashore. During a low tide, seawater gets shallower!

Bootlace worms live in the sandy seabed near the shore. They are the longest worms in the world and can be 55 yards long.

Mangroves are trees that can grow in shallow seawater. Their roots make a good home for crocodiles and young sharks.

Shallow-water homes

Places where the land meets the sea are called coasts. Waves crash onto coasts, shifting sand and breaking up rocks. Twice a day, the sea flows up to the beach and then falls away. These movements of the sea are called tides.

Kelp forests are found in coastal waters. They are homes to the animals that live there.

Animals, such as sharks and seals, live in the coast's shallow waters. Hermit crabs and starfish live on the seabed. Along the coast, there are also thick forests of green kelp, or seaweed, which provide homes for fish and other animals.

Many fish live in the shallow water along coasts.

Waves rise and fall over rocky coasts.

Hermit crabs

Most crabs are protected by a hard shell, but the hermit crab has to borrow one from another animal. Instead of growing its own shell, the hermit crab pushes its soft body into an empty shell left by a sea snail.

Small animals called sea anemones attach themselves to the hermit crab's shell. They feed on the crab's leftover meals.

Sea anemone

Hermit crab

When the hermit crab grows bigger, it finds another empty shell that fits. It pulls its body out of the old shell and moves into a new one.

This hermit crab is looking for the perfect shell.

Hermit crabs have ten legs and two large eyes.

45

Limpets

A limpet is a snail that lives on rocky shores and in kelp forests. It has a cone-shaped shell that looks like a pointed hat.

The limpet moves around using its large foot.

Foot

Starfish pour the contents of their stomach over their prey to turn it into a mushy liquid. The starfish then sucks up the liquid.

Starfish can move at a speed of more than 3 feet a minute.

If a predator pulls off one of the starfish's arms, the arm will grow back.

Octopuses

The octopus is an eight-armed animal. Each arm is covered with suckers that grip prey. The octopus uses its powerful **beak** to rip up and crush the prey into small pieces.

The octopus has two rows of suckers on each arm.

When an octopus is threatened, it releases a cloud of black ink into the water. This confuses the predator, so the octopus can slip away.

An octopus moves by crawling along the seabed using its arms. It can also swim very fast by pushing a jet of water out of its body at high speed.

An octopus's arms can touch, taste, and grip.

The octopus squirts black ink from a tube inside its body.

Garibaldi fish

Bright-orange garibaldi fish live among the kelp off the coast of California. They feed on worms, crabs, and small fish during the day and hide in holes at night.

The male garibaldi fish guards his nest on the seabed.

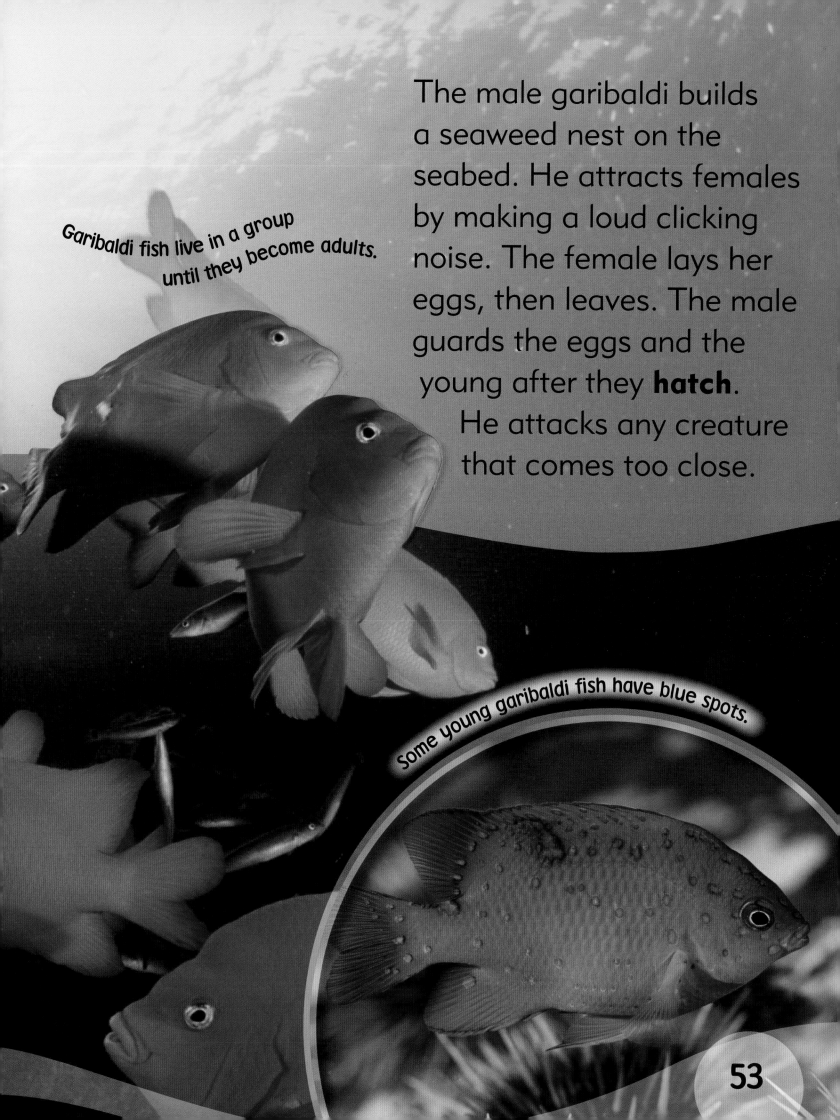

The male garibaldi builds a seaweed nest on the seabed. He attracts females by making a loud clicking noise. The female lays her eggs, then leaves. The male guards the eggs and the young after they **hatch**. He attacks any creature that comes too close.

Garibaldi fish live in a group until they become adults.

Some young garibaldi fish have blue spots.

Spotted trunkfish

The fish has a golden body with black spots. It grows to 11 inches

Spotted trunkfish swim slowly above a coral reef and dart into dark hiding places when they are scared.

There are sharp spines behind the fins.

There are 50 types of trunkfish. This is a cube trunkfish.

When a trunkfish is scared it makes a poison on its skin to kill other fish that try to eat it.

Like other fish, trunkfish breathe underwater. They use their gills to breathe and they use their fins and tail to swim.

Eagle rays

The eagle ray has a pointed nose and a flattened body with huge winglike fins. It swims slowly through the water by flapping its wings. Occasionally, it leaps out of the water.

The mouth of the eagle ray is on the underside of its body.

Spotted eagle rays often swim in shallow water along sandy coasts.

mouth

Eagle rays search for food on the seabed.

The ray uses its strong teeth to crush the shells of seabed creatures, such as crabs and mussels. Its long tail ends in **poisonous spines**, which the ray uses to defend itself from attackers.

Seals

Seals are **mammals**, but instead of legs, they have **flippers**. Their sleek, **streamlined** bodies make them expert swimmers.

Seals are clumsy on land, but very graceful in the water.

Like other mammals, seals have **lungs**, so they must come to the surface to breathe. However, seals can hold their breath for nearly an hour when they swim underwater.

Seals slowly wriggle onto land using their front flippers.

Seals use their front flippers to steady themselves when they are swimming slowly.

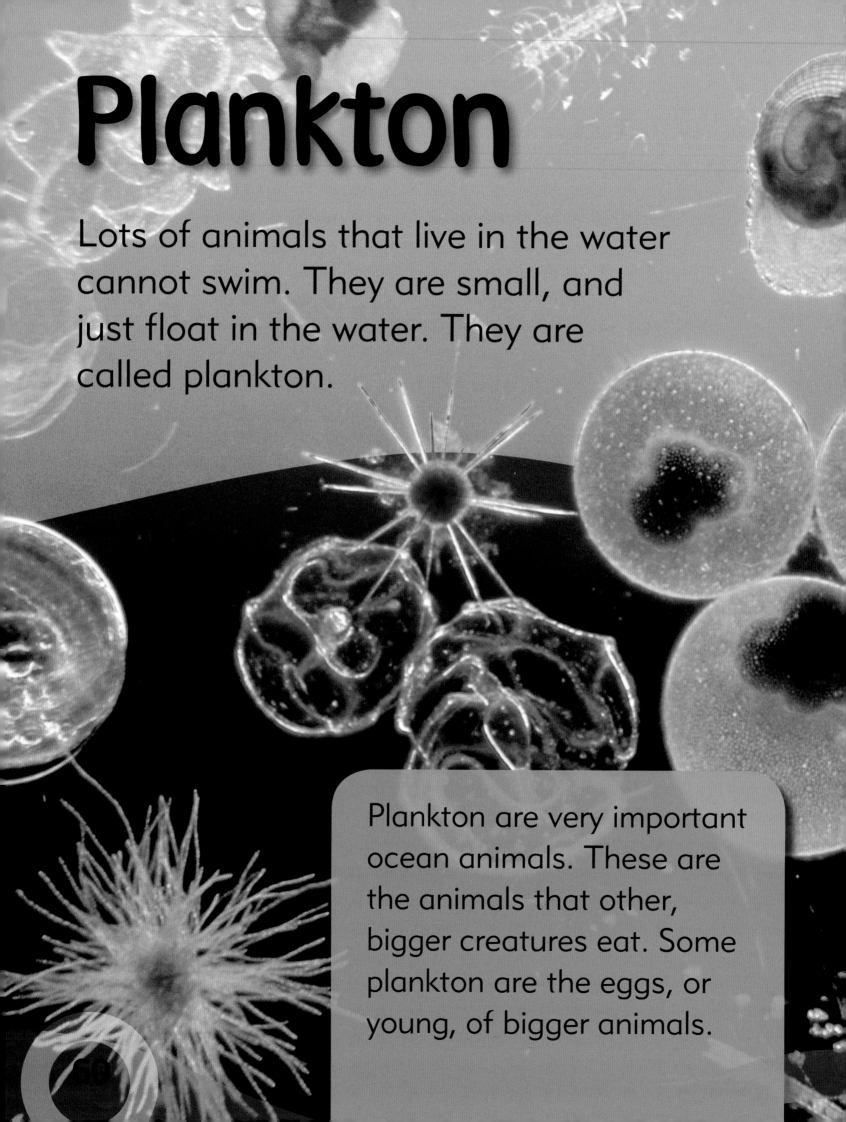

Plankton

Lots of animals that live in the water cannot swim. They are small, and just float in the water. They are called plankton.

Plankton are very important ocean animals. These are the animals that other, bigger creatures eat. Some plankton are the eggs, or young, of bigger animals.

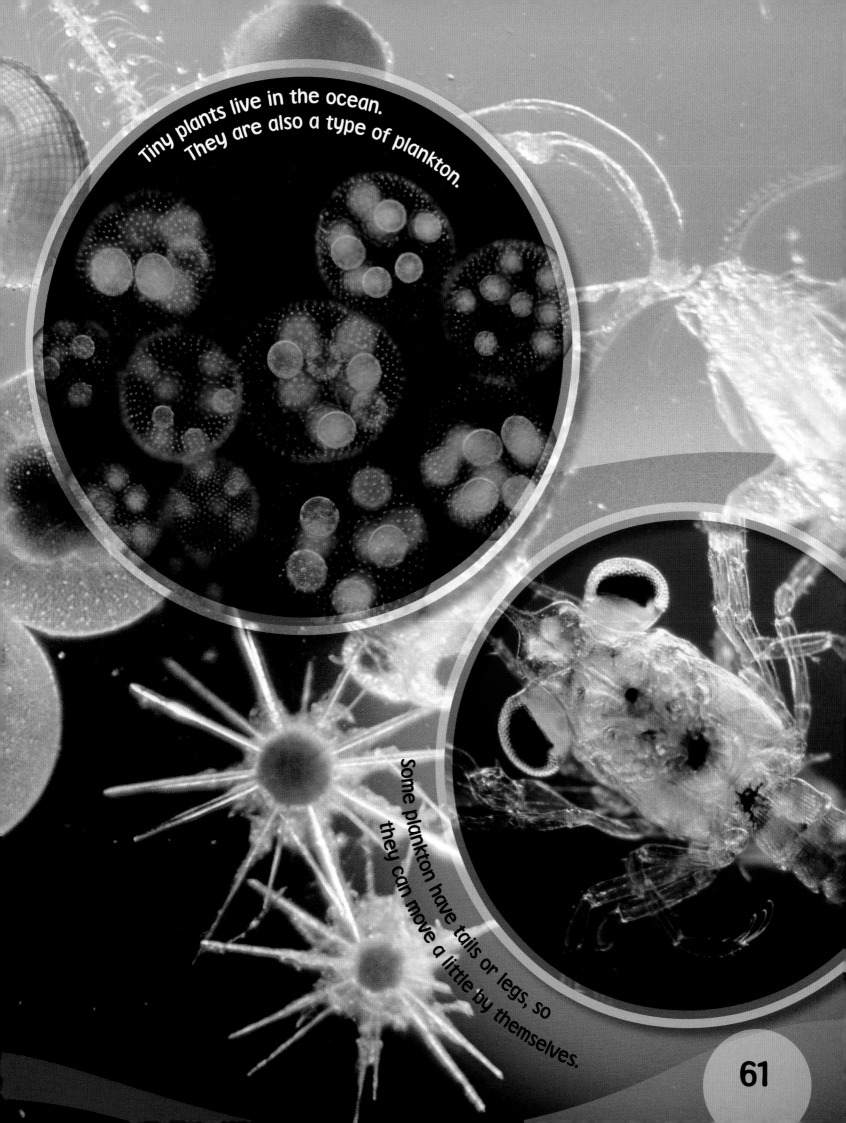

Tiny plants live in the ocean.
They are also a type of plankton.

Some plankton have tails or legs, so
they can move a little by themselves.

Sea horses

The sea horse does not look like a fish. Its body is covered in armorlike scales and it uses its long tail to wrap itself around pieces of seaweed.

Some sea horses are disguised to look like bits of coral or seaweed.

Sea horses wrap their tail around seaweed so they are not carried away by the current.

The sea horse swims upright in the water using tiny fan-shaped fins.

fin

The female sea horse passes her eggs to the male. He puts them in a pouch on the front of his body. He cares for the eggs for several weeks until the young sea horses are ready to live on their own.

Loggerhead turtle

Turtles live in the sea. They can swim huge distances to find food or to lay their eggs. Turtles must lay their eggs on land.

A loggerhead turtle swims to a warm, sandy beach to lay her eggs.

As soon as baby turtles hatch, they scuttle back to the sea.

Leatherback turtles are the biggest turtles in the sea—they can be 5 feet long. Loggerhead turtles however can grow to 3 feet long.

Loggerhead turtles live in shallow water, but when they go on their long journeys they must swim across the open ocean.

Squirrelfish

A squirrelfish has large eyes and its body is covered with large, colorful, prickly scales. Most squirrelfish are red, with yellow, white, or black markings.

A squirrelfish has rows of spines along its **dorsal fin**.

They live near rocky or sandy shores, or coral reefs.

Squirrelfish protect themselves with spiny bodies. They are shy little fish that hide in between rocks or corals. They usually feed at night and hide during the day.

Squirrelfish have large eyes that help them to see at night.

67

Lemon shark

Many sharks live in the deep ocean, but lemon sharks prefer to be in warm shallow water. They swim slowly, but they speed up when they are hunting.

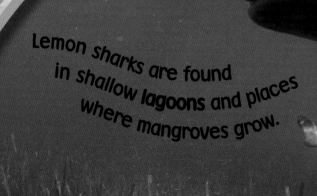

Lemon sharks are found in shallow lagoons and places where mangroves grow.

A lemon shark's skin is gray-yellow. It is white underneath.

Lemon sharks come to shallow water areas to give birth to their young, or pups. The pups stay in the shallow water while they grow bigger.

DEEP-WATER LIFE

The largest and deepest ocean is the Pacific Ocean. It covers more than one-third of the world's surface.

Deep-water snails have lost their shells but have grown little "wings" instead, which they use to swim. They are called sea butterflies.

Sperm whales have the biggest brains of any animal.

The world's largest mountain is in the deep ocean and it is taller than Mount Everest.

Pilot whales can swim to depths of half a mile. They are called "cheetahs of the deep" because they swim fast when they are chasing squid.

Deep sea dumbo octopuses have flaps on their heads that look like big elephant ears.

Some deep sea fish stretch their stomachs so they can eat fish bigger than themselves!

The deep ocean may be dark, but many of the animals that live there make their own light.

Siphonophores are tiny animals that all join up together to make one giant animal, which grows up to 130 feet long!

More people have been to the Moon than have traveled to the deepest part of the ocean.

Deep ocean

People splash and swim on the surface of the ocean, but its waters spread thousands of feet below. In these dark depths are huge underwater mountains and giant valleys.

Scientists explore the deep ocean in special submersibles that take them down to the seabed.

Plenty of light

Light zone: 0-650 feet

Twilight zone: 650-3,250 feet

A little light

No light

Dark zone: Below 3,250 feet

Seabed

Valley

There are many different layers in the ocean.

Apart from the surface layer, ocean water is icy cold and dark. The animals that live here have found ways of surviving in this difficult **environment**.

So far, scientists have explored only a small area of the deep ocean, and they are discovering strange new animals all the time.

The hatchet fish is one of the many strange fish that live in the deep.

Sperm whales

The sperm whale has a large, square head. It lives mostly near the surface of the ocean, but it can also dive into deeper water.

The massive head of the sperm whale makes up to one-third of its length.

Sperm whale calves stay near the surface while their mother hunts.

A sperm whale eats over one ton of squid every day.

Sperm whales can plunge downwards to depths of 6,300 feet or more. For up to two hours, the whale holds its breath and hunts for food, such as giant squid. Finally, it returns to the surface to breathe.

Megamouth sharks

This shark was first discovered in 1976. Since then, only about 40 have been seen. It lives in deep water, where it is dark and very cold.

The megamouth shark is so called because of its huge mouth and rubbery lips. It swims slowly with its mouth wide open. This lets the shark take in massive amounts of water to trap

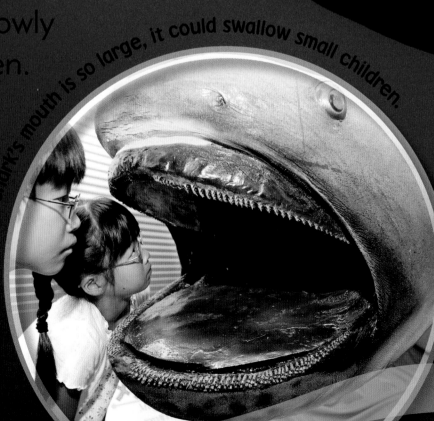

The megamouth shark's mouth is so large, it could swallow small children.

76

Unlike other sharks, which have **muscular** bodies, the megamouth shark has a flabby body. It does not need to swim quickly to catch fish, which is why its muscles are weaker than most other sharks.

The megamouth shark has a large head. Its body grows to about 16 feet long—about as long as a car.

Giant squid

Giant squid grow to about 40 feet long and weigh as much as one ton—that's as long as a bus and as heavy as an SUV!

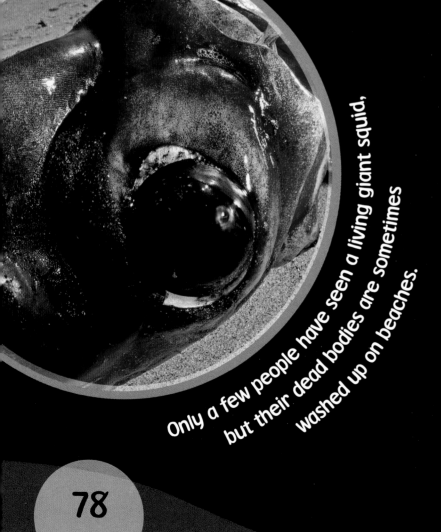

Only a few people have seen a living giant squid, but their dead bodies are sometimes washed up on beaches.

The eye of the giant squid is as large as a dinner plate. This helps it to see its prey in gloomy water.

teeth

Squid have eight arms and two long tentacles covered in suckers. The suckers help the squid to hold on to slippery prey. Giant squid are fearsome hunters and will even attack a sperm whale.

Giant squid suckers are filled with sharp teeth.

Viperfish and gulper eels

It is hard to find food in the ocean's deepest zone. Viperfish and gulper eels lurk in the waters, waiting for prey to pass or a dead creature to sink from the surface waters.

The gulper eel has a hinged mouth that can open wide to swallow prey larger than itself.

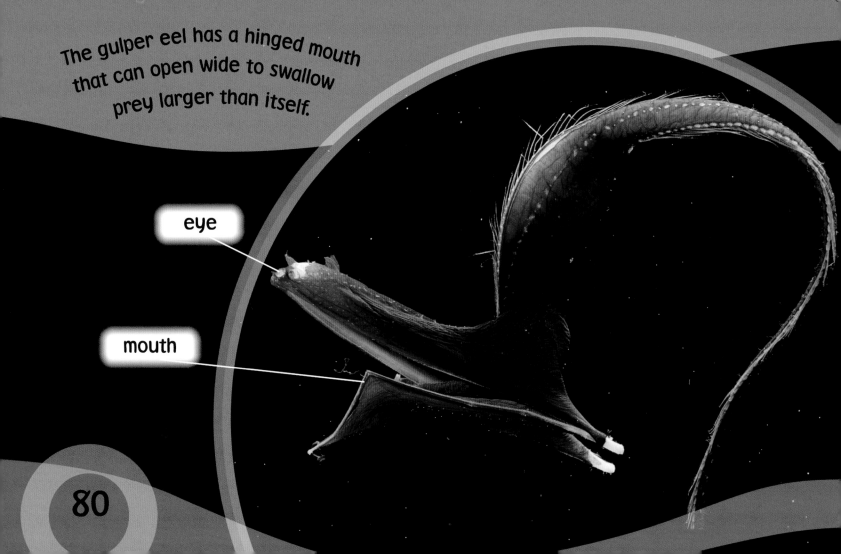

eye

mouth

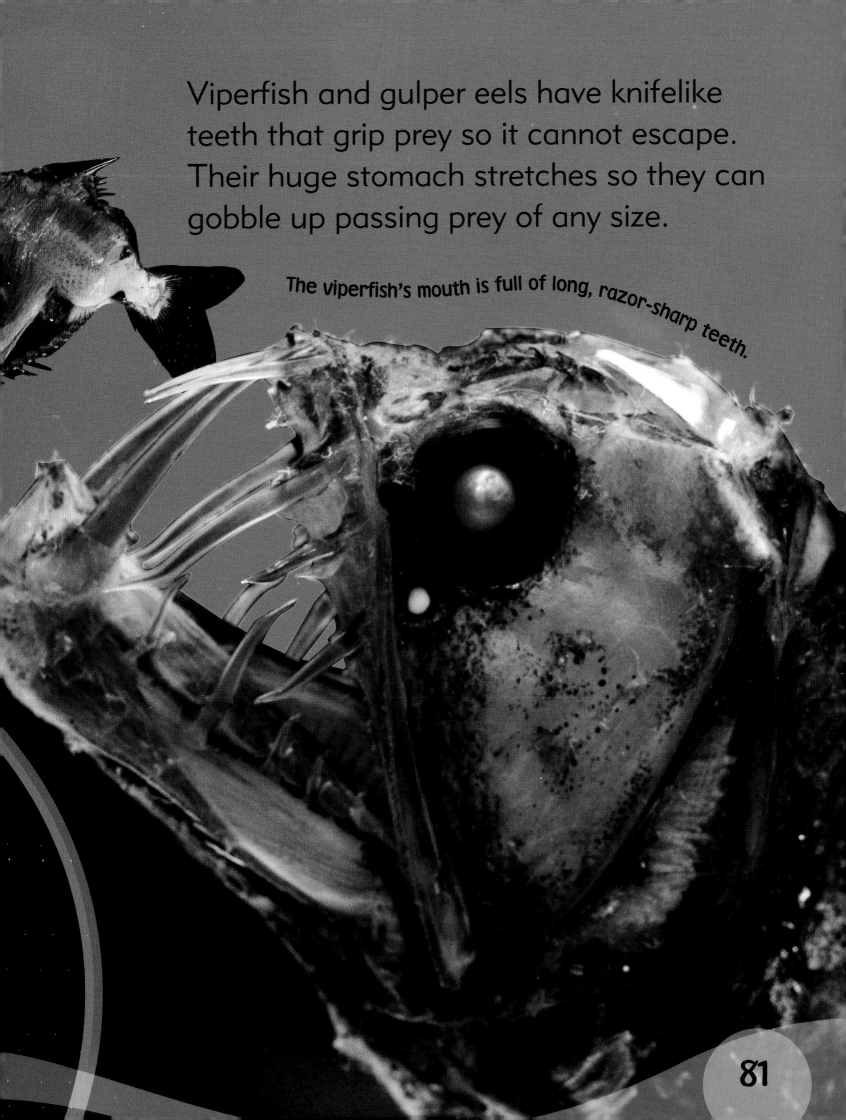

Viperfish and gulper eels have knifelike teeth that grip prey so it cannot escape. Their huge stomach stretches so they can gobble up passing prey of any size.

The viperfish's mouth is full of long, razor-sharp teeth.

Angler fish

The angler fish lives in the darkest depths of the ocean. A long **spine** with light on its tip dangles from the fish's head. The light is made by tiny creatures called **bacteria,** and it tempts prey to come close to the fish's mouth.

In the darkness, other fish swim towards the angler fish's glowing light—and the fish snaps them up.

The angler fish has a huge head and a very wide mouth.

Angler fish can open their jaws wide to swallow fish as large as themselves.

Angler fish have long, daggerlike teeth that point backward. They use their teeth to catch passing prey.

Flashlight fish

Flashlight fish spend the day in the dark parts of the ocean. They swim up toward the shallow water during the night, to feed.

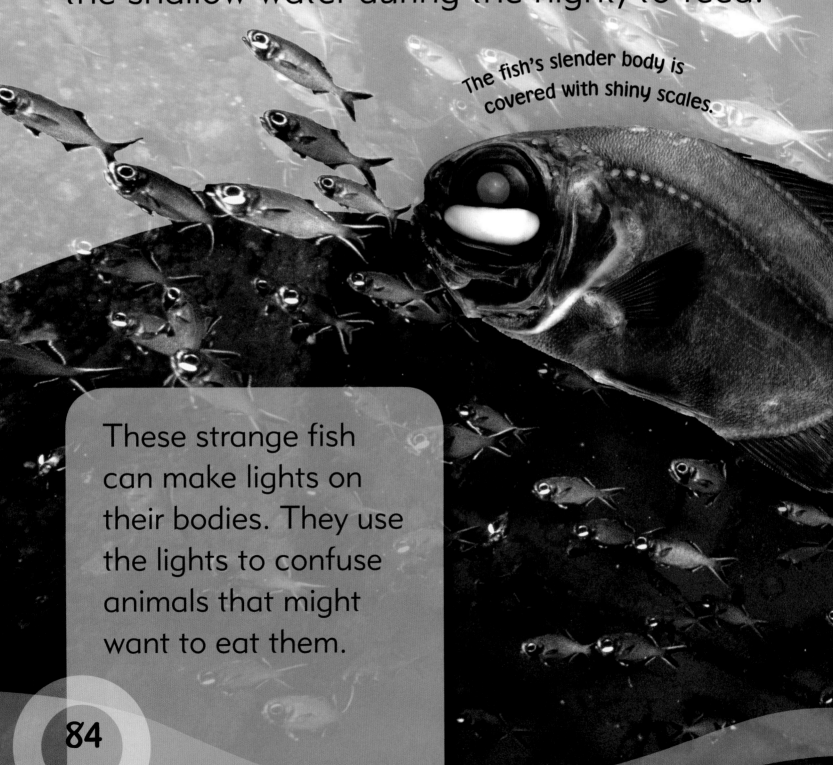

The fish's slender body is covered with shiny scales.

These strange fish can make lights on their bodies. They use the lights to confuse animals that might want to eat them.

Flashlight fish feed on small, shelled animals.

The fish can make light in the skin under its big, oval eyes.

Flashlight fish also use their lights to communicate with each other.

Deep sea dragonfish

This is a fearsome hunter of the deep sea. The dragonfish has a big mouth and huge daggerlike teeth.

A dragonfish looks scary but it is only 2 inches long.

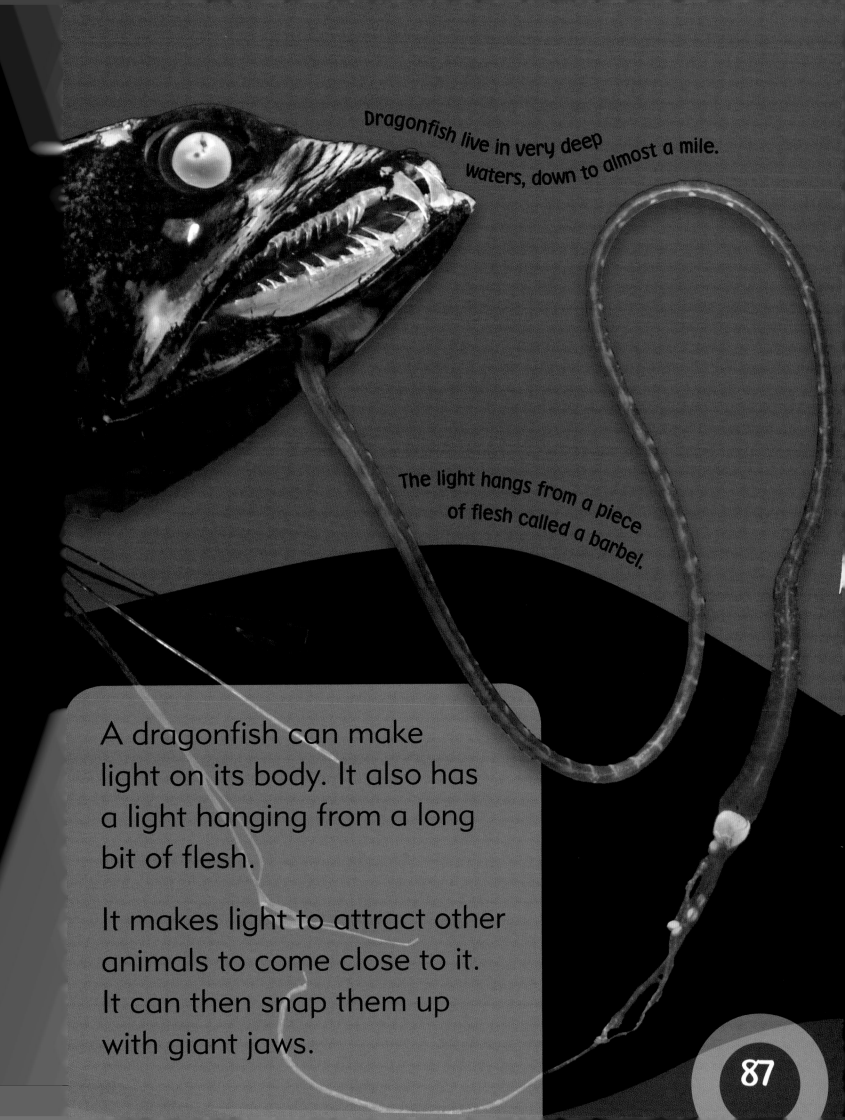

Dragonfish live in very deep waters, down to almost a mile.

The light hangs from a piece of flesh called a barbel.

A dragonfish can make light on its body. It also has a light hanging from a long bit of flesh.

It makes light to attract other animals to come close to it. It can then snap them up with giant jaws.

Spider crabs

Spider crabs have small bodies and ten very long legs. The Japanese spider crab's legs are up to 6 feet long, but its body is only the size of a dinner plate.

In the jet-black darkness, spider crabs use their legs as feelers to find their way around.

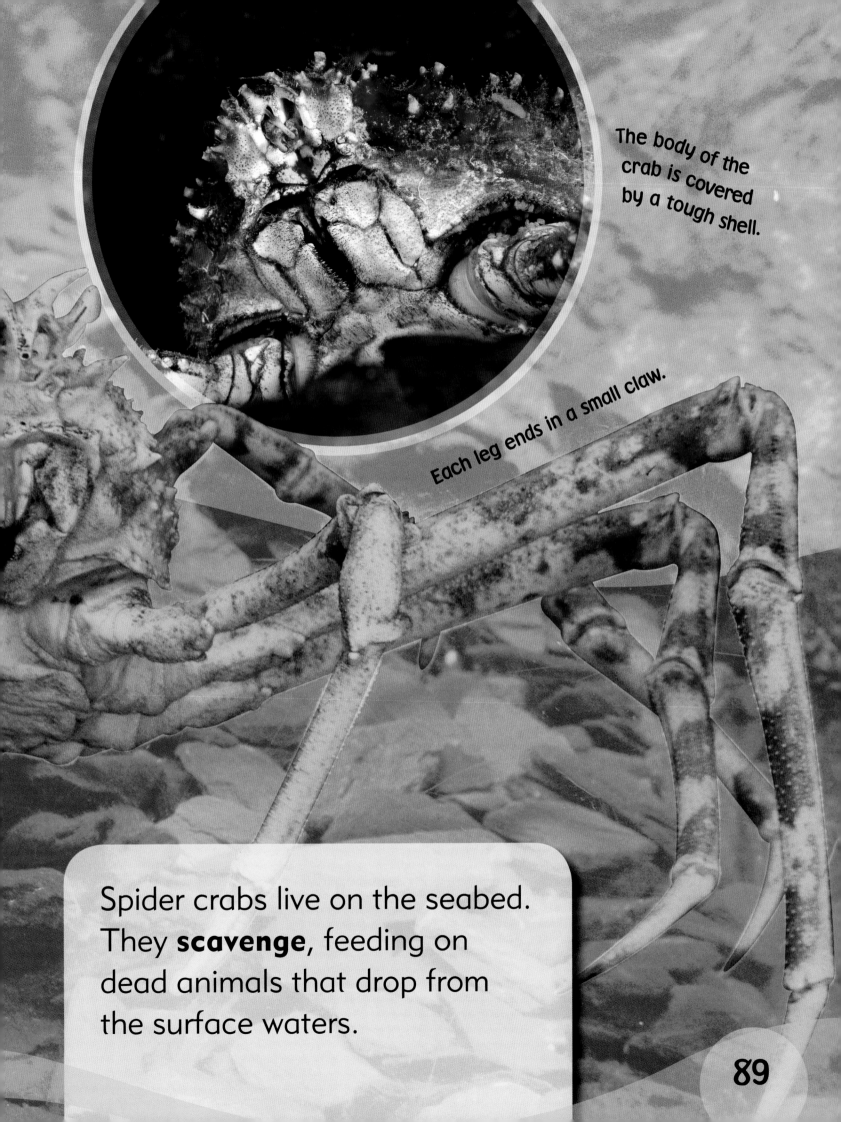

The body of the crab is covered by a tough shell.

Each leg ends in a small claw.

Spider crabs live on the seabed. They **scavenge**, feeding on dead animals that drop from the surface waters.

Giant tube worms

Strange creatures live on the deep-ocean seabed, around **hot water vents**. These are places where extremely hot water gushes from gaps in the rocks.

Giant tube worms live around a hot water vent.

Giant tube worms are taller than an adult person.

Fish and crabs eat giant tube worms.

Giant tube worms grow to more than 6 feet long. They live inside a tough tube that they make themselves. Giant tube worms feed on bacteria that live inside them. The worms are then eaten by crabs and other deep-sea life.

91

Nautiluses

The nautilus has lived in the world's deep oceans for millions of years. It is a type of **mollusk** and is related to the squid. It is called a head-foot animal because its feet (the tentacles) are joined to its head.

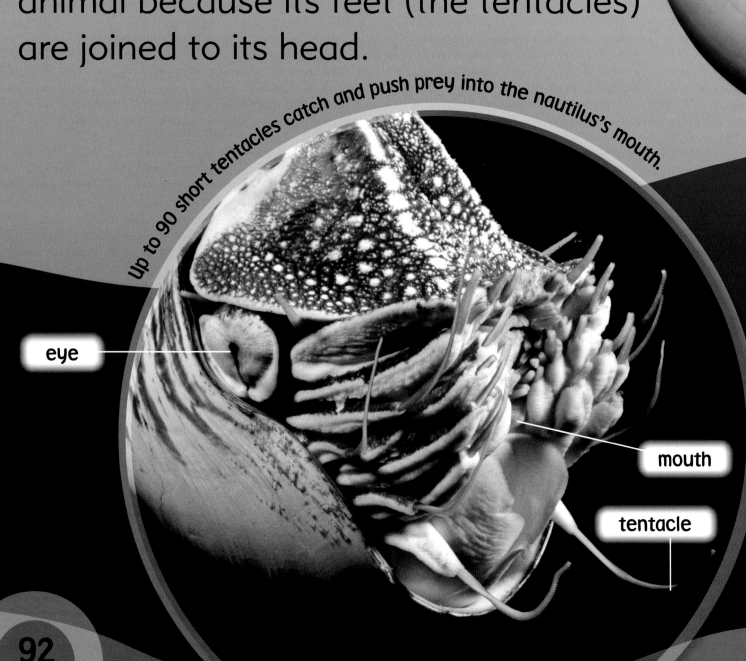

Up to 90 short tentacles catch and push prey into the nautilus's mouth.

eye

mouth

tentacle

Although the nautilus has two eyes, it does not have good eyesight. It uses smell and touch to find food in the dark.

Nautiluses have red-and-white spiral shells, which help to **camouflage** them.

COLD-OCEAN LIFE

Belugas are white whales that live in the Arctic Ocean. They are sometimes called sea canaries because they seem to sing like a bird!

Greenland sharks live in cold oceans. Many of them are blind, but they can still find fish to eat!

Some cold-water sea anemones live for 90 years.

Icefish live in the cold Southern Ocean. They stay alive even when the water around them is turning to ice.

The fastest-swimming penguins are called gentoos. They swim at 22 miles an hour.

Octopuses are very smart. They can learn how to open screw-top jars and reach food inside.

Blue whales are the biggest animals that have ever lived. Their blood vessels are so big that a person could swim through the middle of one of them.

Penguins hold their breath as they swim underwater. They hunt for fish.

Walruses have enormous teeth, called tusks, which they use to pull themselves out of the water and onto sheets of ice.

The ocean's tides are caused by the moon and sun pulling the sea towards them!

In the middle of winter, the Arctic Ocean has no sunlight at all. It is night all of the time!

Cold oceans

The oceans are huge! They cover nearly two-thirds of the Earth's surface. The oceans are deep, too. In some places they reach nearly 7 miles below the surface.

Most of the Earth's surface is covered by water.

Down in the ocean's depths, the water is very cold and dark. Nearer the surface, water is usually warmer because it is heated by sunlight. Most animals live at the surface.

African penguins hunt for fish in the cold waters of the Atlantic Ocean.

Animals of every shape and size live in salty ocean waters. The massive blue whale lives alongside tiny **microscopic** creatures called plankton. All ocean animals are suited to living in their watery world.

Tiny plankton need to be **magnified** for us to see them.

The ocean may be full of many more amazing animals, yet to be discovered.

Orcas

The orca is also called the killer whale, even though it is actually a dolphin. It is one of the fastest ocean hunters. The orca's black-and-white markings make it easy to identify.

Orcas leap high out of the water, then plunge back into it. This is called breaching.

Some orcas stay in the same pod for their whole lives.

Orcas live in groups of about 30, called **pods**. Each pod has its own special language. Orcas "talk" to each other most of the time, so life in a pod can be very noisy!

Orcas will even swim onto the beach to catch a seal.

Dolphins

Dolphins are intelligent and **acrobatic**. Their slim, sleek bodies slip easily through the water. These playful animals often leap out of the water or swim alongside boats.

Dolphins can leap high out of the water. They can also spin in the air and perform somersaults!

Dolphins have small, sharp teeth, which they use to eat fish.

Like killer whales, dolphins swim in groups called pods.

Dolphins use sound to find food. They squeak and whistle. These sounds travel through the water and bump into other animals in the water. This creates **echoes**. The dolphin uses the echoes to work out where its prey is.

Sound

Humpback whales

The humpback whale is one of the giants of the ocean. This huge, heavy animal is also a strong swimmer, singer, and acrobat!

Whales give birth underwater. They push their young to the surface so they can breathe.

Humpback whales jump from the water and perform amazing leaps and twists in the air.

The humbacks talk to each other by singing. Each whale has its own special song, made up of clicks and whistles.

Humpbacks open their mouth wide to take in lots of water. They eat tiny animals and plants, called plankton, that live in the water.

Whale sharks

The whale shark is the largest fish in the ocean. Some grow as long as a bus and weigh a massive 16.5 tons.

The whale shark feeds by swimming along with its mouth wide open. It takes in huge mouthfuls of water, which it sieves through its gills. All the fish, squid, **krill**, and plankton in the water

The whale shark's mouth is 4.5 feet wide, large enough to swallow a child!

Female whale sharks do not lay eggs. Instead, they give birth to as many as 300 baby sharks at one time.

The whale shark has a beautiful pattern of spots on its body.

Herring

The herring is an important fish in the **food chain**. It eats tiny animals and plants called plankton. In turn, larger fish, such as tuna, eat the herring.

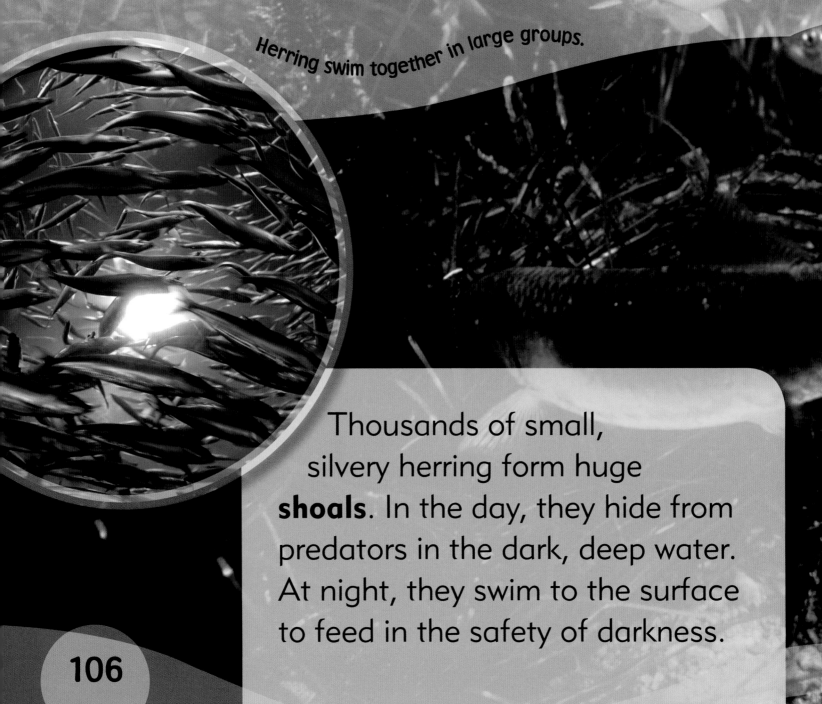

Herring swim together in large groups.

Thousands of small, silvery herring form huge **shoals**. In the day, they hide from predators in the dark, deep water. At night, they swim to the surface to feed in the safety of darkness.

Herring are covered in shiny scales that glint in the sunlight.

Each female herring lays about 40,000 eggs. Only a small number of young herring live to be adults—most are eaten by predators.

Orcas hunt herring shoals.

Tuna

The tuna's long, sleek body is shaped for speed. As its tail fin cuts through the water, the tuna folds back its other fins to create an even smoother shape. This helps it to reach speeds of up to 43 miles an hour. That's as fast as a racehorse can run!

Tuna hunt and eat smaller fish

Tuna live and hunt in large shoals. They swim long distances in search of food. They often travel more than 6,200 miles across the oceans.

The tuna's sleek shape helps it to speed through the water.

Up to 1,000 tuna fish may swim in one shoal.

Sunfish

The sunfish looks like a fish with half a body! Instead of a tail fin, its rounded body flattens at one end. Large fins at the top and bottom of its body help it to steer and stay upright.

The sunfish's large, round mouth is perfect for swallowing jellyfish. Unfortunately, many sunfish die after eating plastic bags, which look like jellyfish floating in the water.

The sunfish's mouth is always open and ready to catch its prey.

The sunfish is one of the largest fish in the ocean.

This massive fish can grow 14 feet tall—taller than two men. It weighs up to 2.2 tons—about as heavy as 25 men!

Sunfish sometimes swim in groups of up to ten fish.

Jellyfish

The jellyfish is not a fish.
It is an invertebrate.
The water supports the
jellyfish's floppy body so
it floats, carried around
by the ocean's **currents**.
If a jellyfish washes up
onto a beach, it collapses
into a soft blob.

A jellyfish's long tentacles trail behind its body.

A group of jellyfish is called a swarm.

Jellyfish live near the surface of the ocean.

The jellyfish's long, hanging tentacles are covered in tiny stings that explode with **poison** when touched. Some jellyfish stings are deadly to people.

113

Glossary

acrobatic able to twist, turn, and jump easily

algae tiny plants that are often eaten by sea animals

atoll a circular coral reef

bacteria tiny creatures that can only be seen through a microscope

beach an area of sand where the sea meets the land

beak the hard snout used to catch prey

camouflage colors and patterns on an animal's body that help it hide in its environment

coral an animal from which coral reefs are built

coral reef a group of hard rocks made of coral

current the flow of water that moves through the ocean

dark zone depths of the ocean where there is no light

dorsal fin the long fin along a fish's back

echo the noise made when sound bounces off objects

environment the area in which an animal or plant lives

fin the part of a fish used to swim and steer

flipper a broad, flat limb of a mammal that lives in water

food chain plants and animals that feed on each other. For instance, plants are eaten by fish, fish are eaten by seals, and seals are eaten by orcas

gill an opening in its body through which an underwater animal breathes

hatch when a baby animal breaks out of its shell

hot water vents openings in the deep seabed where hot water gushes out

krill shrimplike animals the size of your little finger

lagoon an area of salty water that is separate from the sea

light zone upper layer of the ocean

lungs the part of the body that an animal uses to breathe

magnify make something look much bigger than it really is

mammal an animal that is covered with hair and gives birth to live young

microscopic too tiny to see without an instrument called a microscope

mollusk a sea creature, that has a soft body and often a hard shell

mucus a sticky substance made by animals

muscular to have strong muscles

mussel sea creature with a soft body and hard shell

pod a group of dolphins or orcas

poison something that can harm or even kill

poisonous spines sharp parts of an animal's body that can hurt or kill another animal if touched

predator an animal that hunts other animals

prey an animal that is hunted by other animals

reptile an animal with scaly skin that lays eggs

scavenge to search for dead animals to feed on

shoal a group of fish

shrimp a small sea creature with a shell around its body

skeleton the framework of bones supporting the body

spine a long, sharp point

sponge a soft-bodied sea animal

streamlined having a smooth shape that moves easily through water

submersible vehicle used to explore underwater

tentacle a long, armlike limb of a sea creature. It is used for feeling and holding, and sometimes for stinging

twilight zone middle layer of the ocean

Index

Ideas for teachers and parents

- Make a collage of a coral reef. Take a large piece of white paper and draw an outline of a reef, using the photos in this book for inspiration. Look through old magazines and cut out any pictures of fish, sea anemones, and other reef animals. Stick these on the outline to make the reef colorful.

- Look at some of the many websites that feature coral reefs. Some have webcams set up underwater so that children can watch the reef animals.

- There are many partnerships on coral reefs, such as the clown fish that lives with sea anemones, and the zooxanthellae that live with corals and giant clams. Find out more about these relationships and how each partner benefits.

- Look at an atlas to find the Great Barrier Reef in Australia. Find out where other coral reefs are around the world.

- If you live near the beach, take part in a beach litter-pick. Lots of garbage is washed up onto beaches. Conservation organizations often run litter-picks on beaches where volunteers help to clean up the beach.

- Visit a rocky shore to go rock pooling. Make sure you visit when the tide is out, so you can see the rock pools. Look at the different animals, such as small fish, shrimps, and sea anemones. Lots of different snails live on the rocks. Take care when clambering across the rocks and keep a careful eye on the tide.

- Look for more information about rock pools in books and on the Internet. Encourage children to draw a rock pool and some of the animals that live there.

- Visit an aquarium to see ocean creatures up close. Many aquariums have touch pools where children can see and touch animals, such as starfish and rays. At some larger visitor attractions you can see orcas and dolphins.

- Animals of the deep cannot be kept in aquariums. To see photos and videos of these animals, search online. Many documentaries have been made about creatures of the deep. The series can be watched on DVD.

- There are many food chains in the oceans. Use information in the book and from the Internet to find out what eats what. For example, plankton are eaten by herring, herring are eaten by tuna and orca. On a large sheet of paper, draw outlines of the animals. Link them together with arrows to show the feeding relationships. Then color in the animals.

- Ask children to draw a picture showing the different animals that can be found around a hot water vent, such as giant tube worms and spider crabs.

- Visit a fishmonger's or a fish market to see the different types of fish on sale.

- Visit a fishing harbor to watch the fishing boats unloading their catch. You can find out more about the different types of net on the Internet.

- Find out how dolphins are trained to help the navy with tasks including alerting the navy to the presence of underwater mines.

- The ocean is under threat from overfishing, global warming, and many forms of pollution, such as trash, sewage, and oil spills. Coral reefs are also under threat from divers collecting tropical fish for the aquarium trade. Find out more about these threats from books and the Internet.

- Encourage children to think up fun stories and poems about the ocean creatures featured in this book, for the clown fish and its life on the coral reef or the sperm whale and its life in the deep ocean.

- Make a word search using the different ocean-related vocabulary in this book.

Picture credits

Key: T = top, B = bottom, C = center, L = left, R = right

Alamy Images Stephen Frink Collection / Alamy 37B, Cultura RM / Alamy 38, Phillip Augustavo 88B

Corbis Sonke Johnsen,/Visuals Unlimited/Corbis 8, © Norbert Wu/Minden Pictures/ Corbis 8, Nic Bothma/epa 19R Andy Rouse Lawson Wood 28L, 33T, Kevin Schafer 32B, Nic Bothma/epa 19R, Ralph White 90-91, Richard Cummins 88-89, Robert Yin 24-25, Visuals Unlimited 28C, Ed Robinson/ /Design Pics/Corbis 39T,B Borrell Casals/Frank Lane Picture Agency 46, Lawson Wood 49R, Tom Brakefield 56B, Amos Nachoum 105B, Brandon Cole 98-99, Paul A Souders 102B, Stuart Westmorland 113B, Theo Allofs 98B

Dreamstime 3, 14L, 15R, 18L, 24L, 78B, 110L, 110R, 111BL, 111T

Ecoscene 52R, 58L, Phillip Colla 52-53, Reinhard Dirscherl 48L

FLPA Minden Pictures/Norbert Wu 80B

Getty Images Doug Perrine 34, David Nardini 13R, Brian J Skerry/National Geographic 79T, Norbert Wu/Minden Pictures 80-81, 83, Peter David/Taxi 82, Darlyne A Murawski/National Geographic 82-83, Aurora/Sean Davey 106B

istockphoto 12L, 62B, 63T, 99T, 100, 101T, 104L

Naturepl Bruce Rasner/Rotman 76-77

Photolibrary Animals Animals, Earth Scenes 23B, Mauritius Die Bildagentur Gmbh 18–19, Australian Only 75T, Earth Scenes/Animals Animals 78-79, Jim Watt/ Pacific Stock 92-93, Joyce & Frank Burek/Animals Animals 89T, Oxford Scientific 73R, 74-75, 74L, 90L, 92, Science Faction 73L, Toru Yamanaka/AFP 76B, Anthony Bannister/Animals Animals 44T, David B Fleetham/Pacific Stock 50-51, 51B, 56R, F1 Online 58–59, Niall Benvie/Oxford Scientific 46-47, Ralph A Clevenger/Flint Collection 42B, Randy Morse/Animals Animals 52L, Reinhard Dirscherl/Mauritius 44B, Richard Herrmann 59B, Duncan Murrell 102–103, Herb Segars 111BR, James Watt 100-101, 102T, 112-113, Mark Stouffer 107R, Harold Taylor 97, Oxford Scientific/ Richard Herrmann 106-107, 108-109, 108L, 109B, Rodger Jackman 104-105

Science Photo Library Georgette Douwma 25B, Dr Ken Macdonald 91R

Shutterstock 1, 2–3, 6-7, 10-11, 12–13, 14–15, 16–17, 16B, 19T, 20–21, 20-21C, 20B, 21T, 22-23, 23T, 26-27, 28–29, 30-31, 32-33, 36, 37T, 39B, 40-41, 42-43, 43R, 44-45, , 50L, 54B, 55T, 56-57, 62-63, 64-65, 66, 68B, 71B, 96-97, 94-95, 96L, 96R